CENTERING YOUR MARRIAGE ON CHRIST

CENTERING YOUR MARRIAGE ON CHRIST

A WORKBOOK

RICK THOMAS

CENTERING YOUR MARRIAGE ON CHRIST:
A Workbook

ISBN 978-1-966741-09-1

Rick Thomas

Edited by Sheron Wallace

Life Over Coffee
8595 Pelham Rd Ste 400 #406,
Greenville, SC 29615
LifeOverCoffee.com

Dedication

To Dave

Dave Dave Forbes was my friend. The Lord called him home in 2024. The Lord used Dave as a primary means for sharing our work with the world.

I miss you, my friend.

For additional resources, visit
lifeovercoffee.com

Table of Contents

Introduction

What you are about to read is a workbook. I wrote it to come alongside you as you journey the privileges, opportunities, and challenges of marriage. I'm not assuming your marriage is in trouble, but as part of the fallen human race, we all need help, even in preventative ways. I hope you will take the journey with me regardless of where your marriage is. Because this is a workbook, please return to it as often as needed. Like any good resource, you want to revisit it as needed. We know that sin does not take a holiday, so our work is not complete until the Lord Jesus returns and we experience the perfect sinlessness of glorification. My hope is this book will be a significant means of grace as you await the eschatological fulfillment of our salvation.

Thus, rather than moving on to the next good book, consider this one a long-term friend. The Lord can use this resource to transform any marriage if both spouses are willing to commit to its content and the questions that are waiting for them. Planning for several days and dates to do life over coffee may prove redemptive. The most effective way to read this book is to read a chapter together while stopping along the way to talk about the things that the sweet Spirit of God highlights for you. You'll find questions interspersed throughout the chapters for discussion, not necessarily at the end.

- Take your time.
- Talk with each other often.

After you finish a chapter, spend time in prayer with God and have conversations with each other as you work through the reflective questions. May the Lord bless you with the needed hope and help in your marriage.

Rick Thomas

1

Defining and Establishing

If you were helping a couple build a stable marriage, where would you begin? What would be your starting point? What is the main thing that you would want to establish in their minds to help them? Their starting point, also called a presupposition, will determine the kind of marriage they will have with each other. A presupposition provides the lens through which they will interpret, understand, and respond to each other. A couple needs to have the correct presupposition and a practical plan that logically flows out of that presupposition to do life well with each other. Suppose you can help them determine a biblical presupposition through which they can build their life and marriage and construct a practical plan that flows out of that presupposition. In that case, they will be on a redemptive and restorative path to glorify God, benefit each other, and proclaim to the world the goodness, power, and fame of God.

No Other Foundation

We all have a presupposition, a way of thinking about who we are and how we relate to each other. This presuppositional filter through which we see and interpret life influences and shapes the steps that we take throughout our lives. The way we communicate, the motives for our anger, how we think about sex, and our responses to each other are predetermined by our interpretive filter. Imagine a child growing up in an authoritarian familial environment or a new convert getting his religious feet wet in a legalist church culture. In either case, those contexts will curve their lens, distorting their perceptions and challenging their future marital relationships.

Nobody has a 20/20 lens because of Adamic fallenness and other adverse shaping influences, so it's imperative at the beginning of any study to carefully examine why we see, interpret, and respond to life the way that we do.

- What is your presupposition for your life and marriage?
- What is the filter through which you interpret your life and those closest to you?

There are four elements to a presuppositional worldview, with each element building upon the previous one. You can discern your presupposition by examining each element and answering the four fundamental questions that each element asks.

What Defines You?

Everyone then who hears these words of mine and does them will be like a wise man who built his house on the rock. And the rain fell, and the floods came, and the winds blew and beat on that house, but it did not fall, because it had been founded on the rock. And everyone who hears these words of mine and does not do them will be like a foolish man who built his house on the sand. And the rain fell, and the floods came, and the winds blew and beat against that house, and it fell, and great was the fall of it.

(Matthew 7:24-27)

A simple question to get the ball rolling could be, "Upon what do you want to build your life, marriage, and family?" This question is a life-trajectory inquiry. How you answer the question will determine everything else that unfolds in your life and marriage. It will establish the kind of life you will experience as a couple, the career you choose, and your closest companions who will influence your decisions. If you are married and have not had a discussion with your spouse about what you want to build your marriage and family upon, let's have this conversation soon. Make your first life-over-coffee date, including this book, as an opportunity to craft a life plan that answers this foundational question.

If you're about to be married, you're in a great place, with an excellent opportunity to discuss the most important thing you could talk about with your future spouse. This conversation could be one of the most important ones that you will ever have. After you establish your presupposition, you can begin developing a plan that practically executes your presupposition with God and each other. So what about it?

- What defines your life?
- What about your spouse or girlfriend?
- If you have a family, are your children embracing your presuppositional worldview?
- What specific things do you need to adjust or recalibrate to have biblio-centric precision?

Perhaps looking at some of the options—temptations—that define people will alert you to any weaknesses in your presupposition or affirm the clarity that you already have.

- Their job, career, and profession are their presuppositional lens.
- Their family name, heritage, and legacy are their presuppositional lens.
- Their strengths, abilities, and gifts are their presuppositional lens.
- Their money and what it provides is their presuppositional lens.
- Their education and other training are their presuppositional lens.
- Their skin color and preferred ethnic group are their presuppositional lens.
- Their social standing, influence, and privileges are their presuppositional lens.

Does Christ Define You?

So then you are no longer strangers and aliens, but you are fellow citizens with the saints and members of the household of God, built on the foundation of the apostles and prophets, Christ Jesus himself being the cornerstone, in whom the whole structure, being joined together, grows into a holy temple in the Lord. In him you also are being built together into a dwelling place for God by the Spirit.
(Ephesians 2:19-22)

Fortunately, Paul answered the question regarding what should be the makeup of our presuppositional lens through which we see and respond to life. He gave a brief answer, settling the matter once and for all. Jesus Christ is the Person upon which we construct our lives, marriages, families, and relationships. He is the foundation or, as Paul said, He is the cornerstone in whom the whole structure grows. If Christ is not the foundation, then the structure of our lives will not endure. Christ and His Word are eternal, reducing all other foundations to transitory and unstable. As you think about the foundation of your life, make a case for Christ as your presuppositional point of departure.

Should somebody ask you the question about what defines your life, marriage, and family, you can briefly respond by saying your life, marriage, and family are built upon nothing less than the "Person and work of Christ," the gospel. Christ and the gospel are the same; He is the good news. The gospel must define and determine our lives. Every Christian should learn how to build their lives on Christ. It would be a helpful exercise to play the devil's advocate as you consider these matters. If Christ is not the best choice upon which to build your life, what is a better one? By reflecting on the alternatives, you should find yourself firmly fixed on the only correct answer. If someone were to ask you why you are constructing your life on Christ, you can respond by saying it is because you are a Christian, a Christ-follower.

1. I am a Christian.
2. I am a follower of Christ.
3. Thus, I build my life upon Him.

Are You Building Your Life On Christ?

A Christo-centric presupposition is who you are, and it's how you are to live. Let's assume you have been born a second time (John 3:7). If so, you are a follower of Jesus Christ (1 Corinthians 11:1). You do not serve any other master (Matthew 6:24), leading you to conclude that there is no other option for you but to build your life upon, other than the One who regenerated you, gave you His righteousness, will sanctify you, and hold you guiltless in the day of His glorious return. You could be thinking this is quite elementary. Honestly, I hope it is. It would be fantastic if this worldview were true about all Christians. However, it's just not the case. Many gods compete to rule our lives (Exodus 20:3).

For the sake of argument, you know what defines you, and it is Christ. Furthermore, you are building your life upon this eternal foundation. Upon this three-step foundation, you can move to the fourth and last element: Determine how to live practically according to your presupposition. The danger for any of us is that we can articulate the elementary responses, which is our orthodoxy—common sense theology that is nested in our minds. However, when it comes to the practicalization of the gospel in our everyday lives, we find it hard to live outside the academy. I have spent a lifetime counseling astute, articulate academics who knew more about the Bible than me. Their problems were not in the classroom, which can give the impression that we have our lives together. Their trouble was an inability to maintain a reasonable continuum from the knowledge they knew and the lives they lived.

How Do I Make It Practical?

Making it practical is always the challenging part of the Christian life. It is one thing to say that we believe in Christ. Still, it is an entirely different matter to live in authentic, relevant, and practical Christlike ways that have transformative rulership over our hearts and redemptive influence on others (James 2:19). This fourth element of my presuppositional linkage is where many people become befuddled. Some Christians give up at this point because they do not know how to live like the practical Jesus. Though they know that they are to put Christ on display in their lives and that they are to make His name fabulous, there is an unresolvable mystery about how to accomplish this objective practically. The practicalization of the gospel is not as elementary as saying, "I'm a Christ follower."

Throughout this chapter, I have asked you several questions. Before you move on to the next chapter, will you spend time answering each one of them? As mentioned in the introduction, the primary goal is not to get through this book. Neither is it to read once and put on your shelf. Books like these have limited value if they do not lead us into practical transformation. Thus, it's the mastery of the material that I have in view here, not the completion of it. As you collect the questions that I have asked you already, you can add these to the mix.

- Do you have a practical game plan to live out a Christ-centric presupposition in your life?
- Are you and your spouse on the same page in this wondrous pursuit? If not, what needs to happen to recalibrate your covenant to a Christ-centric lifestyle?
- What does your exportation of Christ look like to your spouse? How are you exporting your Christ-life to your spouse? What have been the effects? What do you need to keep on doing? What do you need to change?

Call to Action

1. Please add the question sets above to all the other questions I have asked you throughout this chapter. I want you to spend some time talking with your spouse about what you've just read. Talk to your spouse about your understanding of your presupposition prior to reading this chapter. Share with your spouse a few tweaks you'd like to make to refine what Christ's life should look like in your life and marriage.

2. Ask your spouse to share what they learned from this chapter and why it was important to them. It may be a reminder that they need to revisit and address. Prepare to go on a few life-over-coffee dates so you can have a relaxed, non-distracted discussion about some of the most crucial matters in your life and marriage.

3. Don't forget to invite your spouse into the process. Your spouse is your greatest ally, most avid supporter, and best accountability partner. Please do not neglect this gift, but invite them into this vulnerable space. Hold them accountable for holding you accountable. Make it easy for them to bring care and correction into your life. If you create an environment of grace that convinces them that you must have their care, they will be more willing to step into the innermost parts of your life.

2

Five Core
Elements

I want to lay out five core elements that are practical and replicable in your life and marriage. When practically applied, these ideas can have a transformative effect on those you want to influence the most, starting with your spouse and children. For some believers, the knowledge of the Bible far exceeds their ability to make it practical in their daily lives, especially in their marriages. My appeal to you is not to check these boxes and move on to the next thing but to let each element serve you in the weeks ahead as you practically assess your marriage and make any necessary and appropriate recalibrations.

Modeling

The first and most crucial element of your game plan is to model the life you want to export to others. An excellent way to think about this is by answering the following questions:

- What do you want your spouse to be?
- What do you want your children to be?
- How is your example helping them to become what you want them to be?

One of the most common critiques from children who do not walk in the faith of their parents is how the religion of their parents was not a clear and consistent representation of Jesus. If you want to damage your family, the easiest way to do this is to live a dualistic life. It doesn't matter how smart or successful you are; it's your authentic life, good or bad, that will have the most significant impact on your family's lives.

To encourage your spouse and children to walk in holiness, you must lead them by a clear, pure, authentic, and practical example. Whether you are the husband or wife, or mother or father, you are a leader, and Christ is the picture that you lead your family in emulating. Be like Jesus. Christ was Christ all the time. He was not just Christ when He stood on a hillside teaching large crowds. He was always Christ, even in the lowest of places in Israel. He was Christ before Herod, and He was Christ before the adulteress. You must be like Jesus in the workplace and the home. You must be like Jesus at the grocery store and your church gatherings. There are no days off to not act like Jesus. You are a 24/7 Christian (Christ-follower) all the time.

If you don't get this first step right, it would be best not to attempt to go further until you change. Children respect truth, not liars or hypocrites. Be who you are, and don't try to be something that you are not. If you're a Christian, be one all the time—even in your failures, especially in your failures. Be honest, open, transparent, vulnerable, and accountable. Present to your family the life of Christ. Let them see what Jesus looks like through your example. Modeling the gospel must always precede teaching about the gospel. If you don't model it well, the ones you hope will follow God will reject you and possibly reject Him.

- Will you ask your spouse about the ways in which you are emulating Jesus?
- Will you ask your children about the ways in which

you are emulating Jesus?
- Will you ask your spouse in what ways you need to change to emulate Jesus better?
- Will you ask your children in what ways you need to change to emulate Jesus better?
- If you are not married or do not have children, ask these questions to two or three of your trusted friends who love you and know you well enough to speak the truth to you.

Repenting

Perhaps you think that Jesus never repented. If so, you are correct. Jesus never repented of anything because He never sinned, which is why the second most crucial thing that you can do personally and for your family is to repent every time you fail to represent Jesus the right way. You are not Jesus. Neither am I. You sin. I sin. We sin. And we do it often. Repentance is the only way to continually and consistently be like Christ.

- Would you be characterized as a repenting person? Elaborate on your answer.
- Do you live in a sin-confessing home? Elaborate on your answer.

If you do not regularly practice repentance, you cannot consistently model Jesus—the Person that defines you. Repentance is an area where I failed miserably during the early years of our marriage. It was the first five years of our marriage when I never confessed any sin to my wife. It is a horrible thing to say, but it is true. Though I often sinned against her and God, owning, confessing, and trying to repent of those sins was not part of my Christian life. My lack of repentance skewed the message that I wanted my wife to hear and experience through me. I marginalized my sin—the things I did wrong—and it obscured the picture of Christ. While I would be quick to let her know where she had failed me through her misdeeds, I did not own my sins. I was a hypocrite.

One of the best things you can do for your spouse and children is model repentance before them. Show them how to be Christlike (He was sinless) by teaching them how to remove sin, as observed by your example of repentance.

- When was the last time you confessed your sin to your spouse? How would your spouse answer this question?
- When was the last time you confessed your sin to your children? How would your children answer this question?

If you are not married or do not have children, ask these questions to two or three of your trusted friends, those who love you and know you well enough to speak the truth to you.

Serving

1. **MODELING:** Let's suppose your heart desires to model the life of the Savior consistently.
2. **REPENTING:** Let's further suppose that you are regularly cleaning up your messes by intentionally removing your sin (1 John 1:7-10).

If these things are true for you, the most helpful thing you can do now is do what Christ did: Become a servant. Christ dedicated His entire life to serving others. We see this clearly in Mark 10:45—to serve rather than to be served. His purpose for coming to earth was to serve others (Philippians 2:3-11).

- Would your spouse characterize you as a servant?
- Are you here to be served or to serve?

Your answer to these questions will demonstrate to others if you want to build your life, marriage, and family on the Person and work of Jesus Christ—on the gospel. For example, this quality means a dad does not come home to chill out, as though that is of first importance (1 Corinthians 15:3). When Dad comes home from a long day at work, he is ready to serve his family because this dad knows that he was not placed on earth to be served but to serve. Dad, perhaps you could announce this the next time you arrive home from work. Open the door, step inside, and report to your family:

> *I want you all to know that I am not here for you to serve me. I did not drive from work, thinking I only wanted you to serve me. I am here to serve you.*

This attitude and behavior is what you want to convey to your spouse and family. Why? Because that was the attitude and behavior of the Savior, the one you follow. Jesus was all in on the serving thing, even if it cost Him His life (Luke 22:42). Let your family experience your servant's heart. Let them see you model the Savior as you humbly seek to serve them in practical and specific ways.

- Does anyone in your home out-serve you? Why or why not? See Romans 12:10.
- Do you regularly think of ways you can serve your family members?
- Do you serve only according to your strengths and preferences, or do you also serve in ways that you don't prefer?
- How would your family members (or friends) characterize your servant leadership?

- In what ways do you see those closest to you emulating your example?
- Are they becoming servants because of your example? Please explain.

Encouraging

Now that you've got your attitude and actions in line with the gospel—through modeling, repenting, and serving—it would be good to think about how you can export the life of Christ to others. You want to think about motivating others to change into a similar Christlikeness as yours. Being like Christ and helping others to be like Christ is one of the highest honors, goals, and privileges for any person. I don't know of a Christian dad or mom who would not want their children to be like Jesus. The real issue is how do you help a person become like Christ. So, let me ask, "How do you help a person change their ways?" While there are many aspects to this question, I believe the most redemptive way to motivate a person to change is through motivating with grace. Paul said it this way:

> Or do you presume on the riches of his kindness and forbearance and patience, not knowing that God's kindness is meant to lead you to repentance?
>
> (Romans 2:4)

Paul did not want us to take for granted (presume) the riches of God's kindness, the riches of His forbearance, or the riches of His patience. He knew that it was these riches that led a person to repentance. Paul uses a cluster of words that implies an idea—kindness, forbearance, and patience. You could add more words, like what you see in Galatians 5:22-23, to give you additional examples of the kind of fruit that you want to emulate and employ in your life.

- Do you want a family member to change? Perhaps your spouse?
- Are you using kindness to help motivate them to change? Please explain.
- Are you using forbearance and patience to help them change? Please explain.

Do you remember the context and the method the Lord used to change you? It was the kindness of God that led to your repentance. When you heard the gospel story, you began to think about God's kindness, and shortly after that, you repented (Romans 5:8). Motivating through encouragement should become an often-used means of grace when helping family members to become more like Jesus.

- Would you be characterized as an encourager? Please explain.
- Do you regularly encourage your spouse? Please explain.
- If you have children, do you periodically and appropriately encourage them? Please explain.
- When your spouse thinks about your encouragement or correction, which one would they say you do the most?
- In what ways do you need to change to model the gospel as it pertains to encouragement?

Teaching

This last element is last on purpose because, too many times, spouses and parents prefer to teach their children how to be like Jesus rather than model the life of Jesus before them. Why not? It's easier to send them to a Christian school, Sunday school, Bible study, or some other teaching environment than to give them a personal and transparent example of the life of Christ. This temptation does not mean we should not teach. Teaching is essential, but education should always come from our authentic Christlike example. As you think about teaching your spouse or children, consider the primary way that Jesus taught those whom He wanted to influence. Did He primarily monologue? Did He primarily dialogue?

Jesus spent most of His time teaching in dialogue contexts rather than monologue contexts. The significance of His style is essential. Your best and most valuable teaching time with your spouse and children should be in dialogue contexts rather than your monologue contexts. As you read through the four gospels, take note of how many times Jesus taught through discussion (dialogue) and how many times He taught by monologue—unidirectional. You will find that He was more about interactive dialogue than monologue.

- Are you regularly dialoguing with your family members? Please explain.
- What specific things do you all discuss?
- List three examples of how you taught your spouse through communication. Ask your spouse to help you with this question.
- List three examples of how you taught your children through communication. Ask your children to help you with this question.

Call to Action

Living the Christ life is challenging, costly, and time-consuming. You can't pass your spouse or other family members off to the church and expect them to teach your loved ones how to be like Jesus. A better option is for you to lay down your life for them. Christ came to die, and He's called us to do the same—in an analogous way (Luke 9:23). I'm asking you to make a decision. Will you talk through the questions in this chapter with your spouse? My hope is for you both to assess yourself and each other so you will know how to change uniquely and as a couple.

There are many questions throughout this chapter. With humility, kindness, teachability, vulnerability, and motivation as your drivers, there is no reason for you not to change. Because there are many questions here, it may be better to go on several life-over-coffee dates over the next few weeks to give each of you adequate time to talk to God and each other. I guarantee that if you both humbly interact with each other and with God, He will transform your hearts, lives, and marriage as you walk through these questions.

3

Essential Qualities for Husbands

Every gardener has a garden. Common sense? If you plan to take up gardening, you must have a garden. Another necessary assumption is that it's vital to know something about gardening if your goal is to have one. It is not common sense to engage in the respected work of gardening with no clue about what it takes to be successful at it. When I think about gardening, I always think of my grandfather. He was a master gardener. Though I did not enjoy working in his garden during the hot summer days of my childhood, I never questioned his expertise. The proof was always before my eyes.

A Careful Gardener

Grandpa was a careful, meticulous, and skilled gardener. I'm not sure if a weed ever stayed in his garden for more than a day. From sunrise to sundown, he tended his garden. Though he did many other things with his life, including being the town's meat cutter, he had a particular passion for gardening. He was not obsessive about gardening but proactive and caring. He took gardening seriously, and the fruit of his hands was on full display, primarily at harvest time. He kept one eye on the daily needs of the garden while keeping the other on the future harvest. With the end in mind, he did the day-to-day work necessary to bring to completion his future hopes and expectations.

It's an adage but entirely applicable here: Grandpa got what he paid for because he invested himself in the process. Why am I telling you this? I am reliving my childhood experience with my grandpa because a gardener is an excellent analogy to what a biblical husband should aspire to be. In this chapter, I want to accomplish two things: Envision husbands about their job description while placing the first responsibility of the marriage in their laps rather than their wives. The word husband comes from an old English word, husbandman—a tiller of the soil. We know a husbandman in our day as a gardener, making a husband—in an analogous sense—a gardener.

Proof in the Harvest

If you want to know if a gardener can garden, all you have to do is look at his garden, which is how I learned that my grandfather was a master gardener. The proof was in the bountiful harvest we enjoyed each fall. If you want to know if a husband is a master gardener—that he understands and practices the art of husbandry—look at his garden. His garden is his wife. She is the most explicit and accurate reflection of his gifting, attentiveness, passion, love, and leadership. I am not suggesting that she has no role in her sanctification; that is for later on in this book. The goal here is to highlight the role of the husband, not the non-negotiable responsibility of the wife to love God and her husband with all her heart, soul, mind, and strength as she loves herself.

Whenever a couple comes to me for counseling, one of the initial assessments that I make pertains to the wife. If their marriage is more than a few years old, I want to discern his husbandry ability, skill, gifting, leadership style, and capacities. The most obvious way to do this is by assessing his wife—his garden. She becomes Exhibit A to his effect on her. I want to know how his performance as a husband has affected her. I do not ask him about these things because more objective data is sitting in the room with us. It's her. It's formulaic:

- Husband = gardener.
- Wife = garden.

Return on Investment

We see this worldview more clearly in Ephesians as it pertains to our Savior. He's the model for all husbands, whom Paul calls us to lay down our lives for our wives. Dying for your wife is a non-negotiable essential when talking about the art of husbandry. There are many more things involved in being a good husband, but laying down your life for your wife is high on the list. Paul talked about it this way:

> Husbands, love your wives, as Christ loved the church and gave himself up for her, that he might sanctify her, having cleansed her by the washing of water with the word, so that he might present the church to himself in splendor, without spot or wrinkle or any such thing, that she might be holy and without blemish.
>
> (Ephesians 5:25-27)

We are familiar with the first part of this text—husbands love their wives as Christ loved the church. Though we see what Christ did—He laid down His life—we don't talk as much about what He gets in return for His work. Some unwittingly teach that love is giving yourself to another with no expectation of anything in return, a fallacious teaching.

We should expect something for the work of our hands. The caution comes when we demand it—to where the result of our work in the lives of others controls us—but it's never wrong to expect it.

> (Christ) might present the church to himself in splendor, without spot or wrinkle or any such thing, that she might be holy and without blemish.
>
> (Ephesians 5:27)

Do you see what Christ gets for His effort? He will receive—in some future day—the work of His hands. You could say it this way: He will get a return on His investment. Paul pushes this gospel truth right into the heart of our marriages by exhorting us about how husbands have a responsibility in the overall sanctification and care for their wives. If a husband has been gardening for a few years, there will be objective evidence of his labors, as seen in his wife. These results could be negative or positive, depending on the husband's work and, of course, his wife's cooperation. She becomes Exhibit A of what he has been doing since he married her. If he has been working hard, cultivating the ground of her heart, she will more than likely be responding positively.

A Weedy Wife

No doubt there will be some husbands reading this saying,

> You don't know my wife. If you were married to her, you would not be so presumptuous about this gardening thing.

It would be accurate to say that I don't know your wife. However, it would be problematic for any husband to frame his initial response this way. In my counseling experience, I have never interacted with a troubled marriage where both partners were not at fault. Of course, she has a role to play. It would be preposterous to think otherwise. However, the most likely person to begin with when restoring a marriage is the husband because he is the leader of the home. If a ship is going down, I want to talk to the captain of the vessel first, not his first mate. Too many times, the husband will shrink back from his role in the gardening process by talking about how his wife is the main problem.

This tactic, even though he might have a valid point, is not how any biblical husband should begin talking about the problems in his marriage. If he is humble, he will want to own his role in their dysfunction rather than taking a blame-shifting stance (Matthew 7:3-5). The wise gardener will want to figure out what he needs to do first, not what the plants need to do. The husband should always begin with his failure in a marriage gone sour. I know that your wife has issues. The doctrine of sin informs me about this. My wife has problems, too, but whatever they are, they cannot be my starting point. I mean, who is not messed up?

The Insane Wife

None of us was a prize worth saving when God redeemed us from destruction (Romans 3:10-12). Still, Christ did not look at us and chose to pass on us because the difficulties and the challenges of the task at hand were too daunting. He rolled up His sleeves and began digging into the weeds of our lives. He did this by setting aside His life (Philippians 2:2-6) and dying for us (Romans 5:8). It would be misguided for a husband to begin by complaining about his wife before addressing his gardening deficiencies (Matthew 7:3-5). If you want to grow in the art of husbandry, do not begin by cursing the soil. Begin with your heart.

A wife would have to be unsaved or insane not to respond to a humble man who is seeking to understand her, love her, and lead her (1 Peter 3:7). Admittedly, there are exceptions; some women can be plain mean, but don't be too quick to put your wife in the camp of mean-spirited and insane women. I have met many mean women, but in most cases, being mean is not how they want to be. I am not excusing their current meanness or letting them off the sanctification hook, but I'm also not ignoring the deficiencies of the gardener they married.

The Novice Factor

In today's culture, dads have not trained boys to be husbands. It's almost an assumption that these kids will unlock the mysteries of the art of husbandry after they are married. They won't. The ignorance they bring into their marriages will stay in their marriages if nobody helps them before their marriage. If your marriage is still in its infancy, it would be understandable why you may be a novice in the art of husbandry. It is also understandable that your garden (wife) may need more work than an older and more mature wife. But if you have been married for five years or more, your wife is Exhibit A. She is an objective representation of your love and care. If your wife has a lot of weeds, and if you are not sure how to proceed, I encourage you to find help.

Ask your small group leader or your pastor to give you some assistance. Spend dedicated time learning the art of husbandry. There is no shame in admitting ignorance. We all must learn at some point. By all means, do not become angry, frustrated, apathetic, or disappointed if your garden is not meeting your expectations. Cursing the sun or the dirt is not the path forward. Those responses will not help your circumstances. My grandfather knew how to grow stuff. Though he may have been perplexed or occasionally stumped, he always persevered with a little hope and a whole lot of sweat. A friend of mine recently commented to me that she rarely sees couples who have been married for a while and are still in love with each other. Isn't that a sad commentary on our Christian marriages? Too many marriages are:

- More snippy than playful
- More critical than encouraging
- More hopeless than joyful
- More business partners than lovers
- More like an arranged marriage than a passionate romance
- More like a chore to endure than a union to enjoy

Marriage problems are not how things ought to stay. We have the transformative power of the gospel working in us. We have the Word of God to guide us. We have the Spirit of God to illuminate us. We have the community of God to come around us. The weeds of this world should never choke out the practical wisdom and the power that God provides for His children.

Call to Action

Now that you have the vision, let's make it practical. Here are a few questions I would like for you to think about and apply. If you're a journaling person, begin by reflecting and writing during your quiet times. If you are not a writer, find a close friend to whom you can talk about this chapter. These questions are for husbands, with the hope of changing them first and then their marriages.

1. How would you rate your passion for husbandry, and in what ways do you need to change?
2. What is your general assessment of your marriage, and how do you need to change it to make it better?
3. What tools do you need to become a better husbandman?

4. What are your husbandry weaknesses?
5. Will you go to a trusted friend and ask him to give his honest assessment of you as a husband? What did he say?
6. How much time and in what ways do you pray for your wife? Will you begin praying more for her in specific ways?
7. Write out the fruit of the Spirit in Galatians 5:22-23 and rate your wife in each one of these nine areas.
8. What practical things can you do to help her better represent or model the fruit of the Spirit in her life?
9. Go to your wife and discuss with her what you have journaled and reflected on during your quiet times.
10. Ask her opinion about these matters and pray together, asking the Father for His continued intervening care in your marriage.

In the first part of this chapter, I used all the following words. Write out the first thing that comes to your mind as you think about yourself as a husbandman. After you finish this assignment, go to a trusted friend and ask him to help you change in areas where you need to change.

Expert	Careful	Meticulous
Skilled	Tending	Passion
Proactive	Caring	Serious
Harvest	End in Mind	Daily Work
Future Hope	Expectations	Invested

4

Essential Quality of Wives

One of the most critical questions a wife could ask herself is how she compares herself to her husband. Is she better, worse, or similar to her husband? How she thinks about her role in her marriage and relationship with her husband will determine the trajectory of the union, for good or bad. I'm assuming—for this discussion—that both spouses are maturing, humble, and willing to communicate on the level this perspective requires. If one or both partners are pulling against each other, especially as it applies to a better-than, greater-than attitude toward the other, what I have to say here will not apply. So, how do you compare yourself to your husband?

I Am Chief

Paul answered the "how I compare myself to you" question in 1 Timothy 1:15 when he said he was the most significant sinner he knew. Paul's self-assessment flies in the face of our self-esteem culture, which cannot handle this kind of biblical ego chastening. The irony is how Paul's view of himself is an honest, hope-filled assessment that leads to personal freedom and relational harmony. It is honest because the biblical record is clear—we are unworthy sinners who put Christ on the cross (Romans 3:10-12). It is hope-filled because Christ came to free sinners from captivity (Luke 19:10). Humble admissions to the reality of who we are is the only way we will experience rescue from who we are (James 4:6).

Paul was not discouraged by how he thought about himself. His healthy view became a robust platform upon which he could love God and others most effectively, a platform a wife should operate from to help her husband mature into a God-honoring leader. If she understands how what she did to Christ is far worse than anything anyone has done to her, she will position herself as a powerful means of effectual grace in her husband's life. You see this idea in Matthew 18:32-33:

> Then his master summoned him and said to him, "You wicked servant! I forgave you all that debt because you pleaded with me. And should not you have had mercy on your fellow servant, as I had mercy on you?"

The person that the master was talking to had more significant debt than the fellow he was beating up, but the master released the greater debtor. His question—should not you have had mercy on your fellow servant, as I had compassion on you?—is practically relevant for all of us. We can practicalize it by asking—from our perspective—who is the most prominent sinner we know? From Paul's perspective, it was him. From my perspective, it is me. What about you? Who is the biggest sinner that you know—from your perspective? I trust you would argue Paul and me down from our chief sinner seats, recognizing that you are the chief of all the sinners that you know from your perspective.

Sin Comparing

If we are convinced our sin against God is more significant than anything ever done to us, there is no reason for us to be sinful toward others. Even if we cannot transact forgiveness because the offender is not asking, we should have an attitude of forgiveness toward those who have sinned against us (Luke 23:34) while hoping God will grant repentance to them (2 Timothy 2:24-25) so we can transactionally forgive them. An attitude of forgiveness spills out of the chief sinner's heart, becoming the antidote that keeps him from criticalness, bitterness, anger, and other spiteful characteristics from sabotaging his soul. We can have this grace-infused attitude if we have the correct view of ourselves. To withhold a heart of pity and forgiveness from someone who has sinned against us denies the gospel we say we love (Romans 2:4, 5:8). Unkindness transgresses gospel lines (Ephesians 4:29).

We become idolatrous whenever we step outside biblical boundaries to acquire something we want. Idolatry is an attitude of the heart that acts sinfully to satisfy unrighteous desires. For example, a child wants a toy. It's not an evil desire, but his parent does not give him the toy. The child throws a temper tantrum until the parent consents. The attitude of the child's heart turned evil because what he wanted was more important than honoring or respecting a fellow image-bearer—his parent. The child's behavior too often happens in marriages, and a wife is particularly susceptible, especially if her husband is not learning, loving, or leading her according to her expectations. The blindside that captures her mind is that a desire for a biblical marriage is appropriate, proper, and something she should expect.

Good desires not met put the wife on dangerous ground because she is a hairsbreadth from falling into the unmet desires trap. Suppose she does not appropriate God's effectual grace to her unmet biblical desires. It will only be a matter of time before she becomes critical, bitter, resentful, cynical, harsh, unkind, and full of regret. She will need to do significant soul work, which starts with a robust self-assessment of who she is in light of the gospel's narrative. For example, is she quicker to let herself off the hook than her husband? A common problem is glossing over our sins while lingering long over the sins of others. The temptation is that when a person does not get what they want, they will elevate the unmet desire over any self-righteous judgments or sinful reactions toward the person who did not come through for them. They are playing a dangerous sin-comparing game.

> Not that we dare to classify or compare ourselves with some of those who are commending themselves. But when they measure themselves by one another and compare themselves with one another, they are without understanding.
>
> *(2 Corinthians 10:12)*

> The Pharisee, standing by himself, prayed thus: "God, I thank you that I am not like other men."
>
> *(Luke 18:11)*

Sinning Victims

Suppose we do not see ourselves as similar to others—from an Imago Dei perspective. In that case, we will elevate ourselves above those who disappoint us (James 3:9). No matter how disappointing the other person is, no one is better than anyone else. There is no biblical warrant to look down on another person. Self-righteousness is the heart condition that exalts superior attitudes toward others. God does not bless these attitudes (James 4:6). To sin against someone in response to their sin reveals a person's adverse, albeit practical, walk with Jesus while creating an awkward dualism with the person they sinned against in the relationship. This dualism is the sinning victim construct. Few discipling situations are more challenging than those of the sinning victim. It happens too often.

For example, a wife shares how her husband sinned against her and her sinful responses to him. He has objectively sinned against her, making her a victim. However, she sins against him in response, making her a sinner. It is a delicate process as you walk her through what is wrong with the marriage. Part of the problem is her culpability in the deterioration of the marriage. You cannot move too fast with this knowledge because she will misunderstand you, perceiving you as harsh with your accusation and assuming you do not recognize what her husband did to her. Thus, you begin by carefully—with wisdom—understanding her suffering while sympathetically listening to the hurt and fears she has experienced. Her pain is real. Her story is dark.

More than likely, she is honest and accurate: Her husband has been mean and insensitive toward her. It might be an episode; it could be a pattern. You must give her appropriate time and space to weep over and work through the disappointment that has characterized their marriage (Romans 12:15). You do not want to prematurely introduce more tension into the narrative by addressing her guilt until you have competently, compassionately, and thoroughly communicated your care for her (Romans 8:31). You want to slowly bring her to the place where she can hear the whole truth about what is wrong with their covenant. Your ultimate goal is to position her heart to receive God's help, not just fix her husband.

- She needs to know the Lord is not oblivious to what is happening in her marriage.
- She needs to know God is for her, and He has a better plan for their marriage.

- She needs to know there is no problem where God's grace is inadequate to restore her heart or repair the marriage.
- She needs to know the Lord can use the sin in their marriage to redeem their marriage.

Choose Freedom

These good things can happen if she grieves over the disorderedness in his soul and their marriage while taking her soul to task by fixing what she can about herself. You want her to grieve but not fall into despair. You want her to correct unbiblical thinking but not crush her spirit (Isaiah 42:3; Matthew 12:20). The most common question about the process is, "How do I do this?" The first step is to ensure she is not complicating the problem through personal sinfulness. As you do this, you must discern how God desires to guide you (John 16:13) while trusting Him to work through you to restore her as the precursor to working on what's wrong with him.

If she is going to be a gentle restorer of her husband, she must keep watch over her soul, ensuring the evil one has not entrapped her (Galatians 6:1-3). Don't assume she is ready to be part of God's restoration team when sin is harboring in her heart. It would help if you also let her know that they will not likely simultaneously or equally repent during this season. Their marriage is not a happily-ever-after movie. It's real life. Scriptwriters do not factor in how the doctrine of sin practically works out in our lives. They are making movies, but in real life, every story does not end according to how we want it. We are not in control of the narrative (2 Corinthians 1:8-9). Sin is messy, and there will be times when things do not end happily, with everyone smiling, hugging, and heading over the horizon as the sun fades to black. Families do divide. Marriages do fail.

Christ experienced crucifixion (Isaiah 53:10). Counseling

does not assure preferred outcomes. The husband may never become what the wife wants (2 Corinthians 12:8-9). This potential is where the wife of an unchanging man needs gospel clarity. The gospel can give her what she needs to find restoration, and it can give her all she needs to live in an unreconciled situation with her husband (2 Peter 1:3). There are two options for her:

- If her husband does not repent, will she forgive him attitudinally?
- If her husband does repent, will she forgive him transactionally?

Attitudinal forgiveness is about her heart's attitude toward him—perchance he does not change. She does not want his unrepentant sin to manage her. Thus, the best she can do is free herself from his sin. She can be free even if he never chooses to be free.

No Curve Here

The challenge in an unchanging marriage is whether the victim will do the work to guard their heart against being a sinful, self-righteous person. God does not grade on a curve. Nobody receives special favor from the Lord as though one person is better than someone else; we're all rotten to the core and require His favor (Isaiah 64:6). There are only two grades of people: The Father gives us an F-. He gives His Son an A+. I was a depraved human that God regenerated by grace (Romans 3:12). My good fortune did not come because I turned over a new leaf and became a good person. My redemption and ongoing restoration to God is an undeserved gift from God (Ephesians 2:8-10). I have no right to think my effort makes me better than anyone. If my works are good, it is because God works good into and through me. God is good. Paul could not be more explicit:

None is righteous, no, not one; no one understands; no one seeks for God. All have turned aside; together they have become worthless; no one does good, not even one.

(Romans 3:10-12)

We cannot grade each other on a curve to feel better about ourselves while belittling others. We are bad to the bone. We are simultaneously sinners and victims. Though some sins are consequentially worse than others, we must recognize that any sin is significant enough to put Christ on the cross (James 2:10). This kind of gospel-informed thinking releases us from being controlled by the sins of others, especially by disappointing people who never change. If you understand and practically apply these truths, you will be positioned in the best possible place to help your spouse overcome the things that disrupt your marriage.

I'm not saying your spouse will change, but you can rise above the fray by living a gospel-centered life that recognizes that God made both of you in the Imago Dei. It's never right to sin in response to sin. You can forgive in your heart regardless of what the other person does, and with a spirit of humility, you're in the best place to courageously and compassionately confront, correct, care for, and compel your spouse to change their ways. If they do not choose to change, you will have no regret because you've done all that depends on you to be the most effective spouse you can be (Romans 12:18).

Call to Action

1. Do you pity your spouse as a fallen fellow sinner needing God's empowering favor? If not, why not?
2. Though the consequences for sin can differ significantly, why is it essential to see all humans as equal sinners standing at the foot of the cross?
3. Why would Paul say he was the foremost sinner at the end of his life, knowing others have committed more numerous and grievous sins than him?
4. Why are good desires we don't get from our spouses so deceptive, even tempting us to sin in response to not getting them from our spouses?
5. How are you responding to your unchanging spouse? Do you need to treat him differently when he disappoints you? In what specific and practical ways will you change?

5

No His or Her Problems

There are no his versus her problems in anyone's marriage. There are one flesh problems. Your physical body is an excellent illustration of this worldview. If your finger is hurting, your body is hurting. If there is something wrong with your one flesh marriage, regardless of who is struggling, the whole body is in the struggle. Though you have unique lives, you are one flesh, too. What are the implications and practical applications of two unique people who become one flesh?

A Silly Story

The other day, I was trimming some briars behind our fence in the backyard. I caught my arm on a few of those nasty antagonists. One of the thorns broke the skin and made a slight laceration on my arm. My arm was hurting. It began to bleed. The pain would not go away, so I yelled at my arm. Anger was my way of fixing the problem, which is as dumb as yelling louder at a person who does not speak your language. I lectured my arm because it was inconveniencing me. If only my arm would cooperate, my day would go better. But my disloyal arm would not cooperate. It continued to hurt, and I kept stewing and sulking because of my non-cooperating flesh.

I then had this wild idea. What would it be like not to have this arm? What if I amputated it, replacing it with a better arm? My mind began to fixate on other arms—better arms—as I thought about what life would be like with an arm that did a better job of meeting my expectations. At our church meeting, I caught myself looking around to see what other arms were available. My mind wandered as I wondered. I fantasized ever-so-briefly about life with another arm, a wish gone awry. I felt stuck with this old arm.

An Un-silly Story

Biff and Mable have been married for eight years, and you'd only have to spend a couple of hours with them to know things were not well in their marriage. They were like the man in my silly arm story. The issues that were wrong with them were real, and the stakes were higher because marriage is not a silly, fictional story. There is a disjointedness in their one-flesh union. Neither of them understands how they are ontologically connected and dependent upon each other. They've forgotten how they are no longer two people but one flesh. There cannot be a dichotomy, schism, or fracture in any marriage, but there are those things in their marriage. When you see Biff, you see Mable. When you see Mable, you see Biff. They are one flesh. They are just as one as the man, and his arm is one. They are just as one as the body of Christ, and the head, who is Christ, is one.

Though there are many members in the body of Christ, we are one in the body. There are no competing parts. We all are on the same mission, working the same plan, using our gifts according to how God provides them while putting His name on display. "As it is, there are many parts, yet one body" (1 Corinthians 12:20). Though the husband and wife have different capacities, personalities, strengths, weaknesses, and experiences, marriage is two people coming together to form one flesh for the glory of God. The body never says to the arm, "I do not need you." There cannot be a division in a one-flesh union. Marriage is not a competition but the assimilation of two people who present a dynamic picture of Jesus and His Church.

> For no one ever hated his own flesh, but nourishes and cherishes it, just as Christ does the church, because we are members of his body.
>
> (Ephesians 5:29-30)

Marriage Marathon

This one flesh idea raises a few questions for all married people to consider.

- Are you and your spouse competitors or friends (John 15:15)?
- Is your spouse your best friend? If not, why not?
- How are you working to maintain unity in your body?

If part of your body is rejecting you or if you're rejecting part of your body, you will die, or, minimally, the rejecting portion may need amputation. A body part not assimilating into the body is diseased. Marriage is similar. Spouses spend their entire lives blending into each other until they are entirely and joyfully one flesh, as much as they can be, by life's end. Becoming one flesh does not happen in an absolutely complete way on the wedding day. That particular day is a good start, but it is only the beginning of the marriage marathon. On the wedding day, you hear the starter's gun. The race and all its obstacles and joys are still before you. If you don't understand this, you will be set up for much disappointment as you embark on your marital journey. I've seen this many times with married couples that I have counseled. They fall into two groups.

- I did not know how to have a great marriage.
- I do not care about leading or following well.

I Did Not Know

The "I didn't know how" crowd was never informed, trained, or discipled for marriage. For example, these individuals may have been in a thriving youth group, but that time was not spent getting them ready for the most important thing they will ever do in their lives outside of being born a second time. Marriage is where they will spend most of their lives and most of their energy. Marriage is more important than parenting because if the marriage is not right, the chances of the children being right are exponentially more difficult. Too many of these unaware newly married couples had parents who kept them preoccupied with other things. Sports and other events dominated their teenage years, while little (if any) time was devoted to teaching them how to be what they were going to be as adults.

After their activities fade in their memories or their sport is nothing more than a dusty trophy, the novice couple enters the throes of a long and arduous marriage that they were never equipped to endure. Still, other parents have a myopic college view, as though college is the be-all, end-all. Can I speak plainly here? I counsel more college graduates than any other struggling marriage demographic. I have spent most of my adult life counseling educated and successful couples who are in miserable marriages. Nobody prepared these couples for marriage. Here are three typical responses I hear over and over again regarding the "I did not know how" crowd.

- I never knew. My dad never taught me these things, and my church didn't do it either. A biblical marriage is new to me.
- I had no idea how to lead or shepherd my wife.

- These ideas are foreign to me. This counseling season is the first time someone has taken me aside and practically taught me what it means to bring the gospel to bear in my marriage.

I Do Not Care

Another people group is those who don't care about leading or following well. Getting a wife was just one of the many to-do's on their list of goals. For some individuals, getting married is better than being single, and their wedding day is the beginning and end of their marriage goals. The similarity between this group and the "I didn't know how" group is that nobody envisioned either group for marriage. The former group was mostly ignorant, while the latter group was primarily selfish. There is a slight difference. The uncaring man has the conquer and move-on mindset. He got the girl, and now it's time to pursue other trophies. He secures a wife, a job, and whatever the next thing is as he chases his dreams.

He doesn't give his wife much thought unless he needs her to do something for him. He lives as though there is no need for ongoing marriage maintenance. His views are about himself. His wife makes a similar mental marital misfire, thinking he will act like an adult. She assumes what an adult should be and maps that expectation over her husband. It does not dawn on her that he may have pre-problems and is in need of her discipleship care. It's easy for a wife to misunderstand her full role in marriage, specifically as a disciple-maker for her husband. An added complication might be that she cared about the marriage during the early years, but she experienced weakened perseverance at some point, and she turned to her children as an escape from her unfulfilled marriage dream.

Marriage and Sin

Be sober-minded; be watchful. Your adversary the devil prowls around like a roaring lion, seeking someone to devour.

(1 Peter 5:8)

Both of these groups have a weak view of the doctrine of sin. They don't see sin as cancer that is seeking to devour whomever it can tempt, lure, and capture (James 1:14-15). They misunderstand the nature of sin and their mutual, complementary roles in marriage. Christian marriage partners are co-inheritors of the gift of life. They are not competitors. They continually assess, observe, care for, teach, and uniquely complement each other for the glory of God.

Likewise, husbands, live with your wives in an understanding way, showing honor to the woman as the weaker vessel, since they are heirs with you of the grace of life, so that your prayers may not be hindered.

(1 Peter 3:7)

The maturing couple understands the nature of sin and their complementary roles in their marriage. They see sin as their ever-encroaching adversary and the marriage as their God-given opportunity to defeat it together. This reality is why discerning couples are considerate, aware, caring, and eager to disciple each other. The husband does not assume everything is okay and ongoing maintenance is not needed. His wife is similar. She is considerate of her husband's weaknesses and eagerly seeks to speak into those weaknesses, knowing they are not competing with each other but are one flesh friends.

Mutual Pain and Gain

There are no his versus her problems in marriage. There is only one problem, one marriage, and one opportunity. May I illustrate? I watched my wife go through three miscarriages. They happened to her. It was her pain, her disappointment, her fear. They were my miscarriages, too. I did not feel or hurt the way she did. I have no idea of the physical, mental, and emotional agony of a miscarriage—at least not the way she does. But I hurt because she was hurting. I hurt because I lost something, too. We are one flesh. When someone murdered my brother in 1997, my wife hurt along with me. She did not hurt the way I did, but she hurt because her husband was suffering. We are not two people acting independently of each other. We are one body.

> Remember those who are in prison, as though in prison with them, and those who are mistreated, since you also are in the body.
>
> (Hebrews 13:3)

- Do you hurt when your spouse is hurting?
- What hinders you from entering into your spouse's pain?
- What will it take for you to do for your spouse what Christ did for you (Matthew 18:33)?
- What is your biblical responsibility regarding your spouse's sin?

When I sin—no matter what it is—my wife has a responsibility for that sin. She would never say, "That's Rick's problem. That's his sin." No, it's our sin. She is not guilty of my sin, and she does not repent of my sin, but she has a role to play because she is me, and I am her—we are one. When I sin, she runs to my aid by calling me out and caring for me. She becomes my discipler, my confidant. Just like when the briar cuts the arm, the body comes to the rescue. Too many times, when one marriage partner sins, the other acts like my silly story at the beginning of this chapter. The wife acts as though she is not part of the body and it's the husband's problem. This attitude is the Job's wife syndrome: The non-sinning spouse gets mad when the other spouse sins (Job 2:9).

Ironically (and biblically), this means both of them are sinning. When two people respond sinfully to sin, they both are guilty before God and before each other. They both need to repent. It's like cursing your arm when it gets cut. That's weird. That's your body. You shouldn't get mad at yourself when something happens to you. Are you following my logic? It is biblical insanity to choose sinful anger at your spouse when they sin. When part of the body rejects another part of the body, you have a problem. You better call a doctor, or, in this case, if you're unwilling to repent, you better call your pastor, elder, small group leader, or some other competent helper in your church because you need it. There is something wrong with your body.

Rescue or Accuse

Are you a rescuer and restorer, or are you a critic and condemner? You'll never be more tested on this than when your spouse does something that hurts you. Your spouse is an instrument the Lord uses to measure and mature you. We see this in Paul's warning about a person in sin and a person who helps a person in sin. Take a look at these three verses and note how much time Paul spent talking to the helper rather than the person in sin. Paul gives us seven words regarding the person in sin and forty-seven words for the person who is supposed to help the person in sin. This difference is no small matter. We should read this as a warning.

Brothers, if anyone is caught in any transgression, you who are spiritual should restore him in a spirit of gentleness. Keep watch on yourself, lest you too be tempted. Bear one another's burdens, and so fulfill the law of Christ. For if anyone thinks he is something, when he is nothing, he deceives himself.
(Galatians 6:1-3)

If you don't see your spouse's problem as your problem and don't actively become part of the solution, your marriage will go to places where it cannot recover. Paul warned the restorers in Galatia to guard their hearts against this kind of self-deception, and if you do, you will fulfill the law of Christ, which in this verse means bearing each others' burdens.

Call to Action

1. What are some areas where your husband is weak and needs your help?
2. What are some areas where your wife is weak and needs your help?
3. When your spouse sins, are you envisioned and ready to restore your spouse? Or, are you more apt to sin against your spouse, similar to my silly story at the beginning?
4. Are you a burden-bearer for your spouse? In what ways do you need to change to be a better burden-bearer? Will you write out those ways and talk to your spouse about how you need to change?

Conclusion

Thank you for reading this book. I trust that you have gleaned many new ideas or been reminded of things that you want to apply to your life and marriage. I hope you were simultaneously convicted and encouraged throughout this book. Convicted about areas that need to change in your life and marriage, and encouraged where you have already been appropriating the Lord's grace into your lives. As noted at the beginning, this book is a workbook intended to have residual, practical, and transformative benefits. Here are a few final thoughts for your consideration.

- Have you worked through all the questions?
- What is your specific plan to make this resource come alive in your marriage?
- What is one thing you will do next?
- Will you share that specific thing with your spouse?

Let a close friend know about your and your spouse's plans and ask this person to participate in the process. Finally, don't forget to check out the many other resources in our coffee shop, LifeOverCoffee.com.

Rick Thomas

About the Author

 Rick Thomas launched the Life Over Coffee global training network in 2008 to bring hope and help for you and others by creating resources that spark conversations for transformation. His primary responsibilities are resource creation and leadership development, which he does through speaking, writing, podcasting, and educating. In 1990 he earned a BA in Theology and, in 1991, a BS in Education. In 1993, he received his ordination into Christian ministry, and in 2000, he graduated with an MA in Counseling from The Master's University. In 2006, he was recognized as a Fellow of the Association of Certified Biblical Counselors (ACBC).